Wonder, Lust & Itchy Feet

In **WONDER, LUST & ITCHY FEET** a fearless, intelligent and eager woman—mother, lover, wife and daughter—collects for the first time a selection of poetry from her first four decades of living and writing. Unhesitatingly she exposes intimate feelings and heartfelt values about friendship, family, desire, disaster, finding a home and exploring the world.

There is disappointment and rebellion here; but also humour and wisdom. There is passion, pain, regret, hope; a desire to love and live to the full. The work feels powered by a desire to find life's joy, knowing that tomorrow we die; yet there is also a generous understanding that a new generation will take our place, live and love in their turn.

Sally Dellow's deliberate use of simple language provides a counterpoint to her sophistication of structure, delightful and meaningful word-play, and entertaining rhyme. There is a wide range of reference garnered from rich experience of life and travel in many cultures and countries.

As a poet, Sally Dellow has a highly intelligent understanding of the right words and concepts to express, and communicate effectively, deep-felt universal experiences in a highly personal way. Among the many striking and strong poems in this collection, 'Sand' is one that has the resonance of a modern classic.

SALLY DELLOW grew up in Germany, Cyprus and Australia, the second of three daughters born to an English military officer and a Welsh teacher. She attended twelve schools in thirteen years before studying law at King's College, University of London. A year as a London commuter put her off settling in the UK, so she left with a backpack, a one-way ticket to New York and US$100 hidden in her left boot! She spent two years traveling and working (receptionist in an old folks' home, toilet cleaner, paging telephonist, milkshake maker...) through North America, Fiji, New Zealand, Australia and South East Asia before finally arriving in Hong Kong—which has been her home since 1989.

With her second husband, Paul (an ornithologist), Sally has two children, Eliza and Flynn. She writes around the demands of her busy career running Dramatic Difference, a consultancy through which she works for corporate clients as an Executive Coach and Facilitator, and heads a team of professional Roleplayers working primarily in assessment and development interventions. Also an actor and playwright, Sally has staged her adaptation of C.S. Lewis's *The Magician's Nephew*, and four original works in Hong Kong: *Labour of Love, Pinocchio—A Pantomime* (with Steven Lewis), *Making Boobs* and *Dreams in Sight*.

Sally's poetry has appeared in the anthologies *OutLoud, PoetryLive!* and *Not A Muse*; she has also published pieces in the *Asia Literary Review* and online through the *Asia-Pacific Writers Network*. She particularly loves performing her poetry and has taken it from page to stage at the Hong Kong Fringe Festival, OutLoud and the Man Hong Kong International Literary Festival.

A Proverse Prize Publication

Wonder, Lust & Itchy Feet

Sally Dellow

Proverse Hong Kong

Wonder, Lust & Itchy Feet
by Sally Dellow
Alternate edition published in Hong Kong by Proverse Hong Kong, March 2019
ISBN: 978-988-8491-61-2
Copyright © Proverse Hong Kong March 2019
First published in Hong Kong by Proverse Hong Kong 22 November 2011
ISBN: 978-988-19932-7-4
Copyright © Proverse Hong Kong 22 November 2011

The following are quoted by kind permission of the copyright owners:
DANNY SCHEINMANN: "RANDOM ACTS OF HEROIC LOVE",
Copyright © 2007 Danny Scheinmann.
CAROL SHIELDS: "UNLESS". Copyright © 2002 Carol Shields",
First published in 2002 in Great Britain by Fourth Estate,
First published in 2002 in Canada by Random House Canada,
First published in 2002 in the USA by HarperCollins Publishers.

Cover photography by Peter Inglis
Cover and page design by Shane Drever and Nicole Graham
Printed in Hong Kong by Artist Hong Kong Company, Unit D3, G/F, Phase 3, Kwun Tong Industrial Centre, 448-458 Kwun Tong Road, Kowloon, Hong Kong.

Distribution (Hong Kong and Worldwide):
The Chinese University Press of Hong Kong, The Chinese University of Hong Kong, Shatin, New Territories, Hong Kong, SAR.
www.chineseupress.com; Email: cup@cuhk.edu.hk
Tel: (INT+852) 2609-6508; Fax: (INT+852) 2603-7355

Distribution and other enquiries: Proverse Hong Kong, PO Box 259,
Tung Chung Post Office, Tung Chung, Lantau, NT, Hong Kong SAR

Proverse Hong Kong

British Library Cataloguing in Publication Data (1st edition)
Dellow, Sally.
Wonder, lust & itchy feet.
I. Title
821.9'2-dc23

ISBN-13: 9789881993274

Foreword

Sally Dellow and I have been friends and fellow members of the Hong Kong "Outloud" poetry group for many years. I have read with Sally, and listened to her deliver her unique work with a flair and clarity that is the envy of many of her contemporaries. I declare a partisan affinity; I am a fan.

Sally is a special poet whose work makes an impact whether it is heard in performance or read as the printed word. I well recall a reading of her poem 'Sand' at a literary festival event for students, where half the room was in tears at the end. She has an uncanny ability to cut through to the heart of a subject and not only to paint a vivid mental picture but also to evoke the appropriate emotion.

Poetry has been described as "The right words in the right order" and Sally has a great ability to choose and order the right words, words that chime with other words, words that rhyme and dance in rhythm, words with connotations, alliterations and ramifications.

In this first collection, Sally writes her life (and sometimes others' lives). She carefully navigates the interstices between laughter and tears, between restlessness and home-making, between love goddess and earth mother. Not a poet given to flowery impressionistic vagueness, she shares, eloquently, life experiences that we have all been through at some time.

Great poetry is not the unveiling of new information, but the restating of old recognisable themes in a way that we ourselves could never state. In this way we walk, not in another's shoes, but perhaps wearing their socks, or sometimes in Sally's case, an item of her lingerie!

Wonder, Lust & Itchy Feet is an intimate journey; the emotional vulnerability gives the pieces veracity. Tellingly, many Hong Kong poems in the Itchy Feet section declare her commitment to the place she has made her home. Perhaps she has scratched that itch for the last time.

David McKirdy
Author of *Accidental Occidental*

For Eliza & Flynn: I love you

My past
Our present
Your future

Author's Introduction and Acknowledgements

As I thought about creating this book, I looked back through my "body of work". My poems sorted themselves naturally into three broad themes. The first and most obvious theme was sensuality: sex, skin, love, laughter, wine, dancing, passion; what I think of as "lust for life". This became Part 2: Lust.

The second theme was travel. I grew up moving around the world and continue to travel often and with gusto, frequently responding to places in rhyme or rhythm. In fact, too long in the same place and I experience itchy feet—hence the title for Part 3.

The wordplay of "wanderlust" and "itchy feet" led me to the title "Wonder" for Part 1. The word seemed appropriate for this looser collection of poems that address the successes, surprises, foibles and failings in my world, in my life and in the lives (real and perceived) of the circles that surround me. "Wonder" also captures my curiosity, my love of novelty, and my belief that the world is ultimately a kind, loving and "wonder-full" place.

I thank Verner and Gillian Bickley, Nicole Graham and Shane Drever for their skill in creating these pages. Peter Inglis, Martin Alexander, David Hill, Viki Holmes and Thad Rutkowski receive stars on the pavement of my life for giving their time and creative comradeship. To Danny Scheinmann, Donald Shields, Bella Pomer, Melis Dagoglu, Kara Bristow, Professor Richard Dury and Edina Imrik I express my delight at the generosity of strangers who lit lanterns along the dark paths through the forest of rights and permissions.

Family and friends (particularly my mummy and Paul) have supported me and my poetry for decades—thank you, my loves. And a special hug to Mr McKirdy for the inspirational nagging that drove me finally to publish this book.

Sally Dellow

Table of Contents

Early Responses to *Wonder, Lust & Itchy Feet* 152

WONDER

"The world is so full of a number of things, I'm sure we should all be as happy as kings."

—Robert Louis Stevenson
'Happy Thought', *A Child's Garden of Verse*

A Moment Before Manhood

My son. My little boy. My magical mystery tour.
Golden child:
Emperor of the realm of sandals, sunhats and superheroes,
Daily victor over vocabulary,
Proud digger-up of pirate treasure.
With what pleasure
I watch you.

Your towers of blocks,
Your tumbles and knocks,
The cuddles and kisses,
Attempts and near-misses,
As you build your doorway to manhood.

No measure, no scale, can weigh the love,
Golden child,
When you bring me your banged knees, your broken
swords.
Courageous explorer of minefields,
Feisty finder of pleasure and pain—
Again and again
I watch you.

Your towers of blocks,
Your tumbles and knocks,
The cuddles and kisses,
Attempts and near-misses,
That build your doorway to manhood.

21st century third-cultured boy, I feel such joy
As stroke by stroke
I watch you write your character.
And more so
When you're bored so
You break off and construct yourself
From dinosaurs and Lego.

Your towers of blocks,
Your tumbles and knocks,
The cuddles and kisses,
Attempts and near-misses,
Building your doorway to manhood.

Time extends in an unbroken line
From me and mine
Into a future that is you and yours.
What more could any mother ask
Than the chance
To be near you, to watch you
And cheer you from the sidelines of your life;
To applaud as you pass away from me,
Through your doorway to manhood.

For FJWL.

• Wonder

Age

When all my laughter lines
Join hands
With all my frowns,
And I offset my minor triumphs
Against
My major let-downs;
When warp and weft of once-brown
Hair weave grey
Across my head...
I'll know that I am on my way
To getting old,
Then dead.

At the Breast

You take my body completely,
Indiscreetly;
Consuming me,
Presuming upon me without thought.

You expose me to public scrutiny,
Inscrutably
Watching me react
As you touch me, intimately, at whim.

You want me unceasingly,
Increasingly,
Seizing me
And using me to satisfy your needs.

Yet I offer myself up to you willingly.
Thrillingly,
I feel you
Loving me more with every mouthful.

Badge of Office

A line of ladies wearing name tags;
A professional conference takes a break for the loo.
"Fuck the real world, I'm an artist":
Wearing my badge proudly, I join the queue.

Beware

Beware those who read too much into too little...
And decipher discord in difference.

It's nearly midnight
And I climb into bed, thinking,
Why is it that
When you're out drinking, gadding,
While I stay home, padding about the house,
Tending the baby,
Keeping watch,
That when I finally get to
Sleeping, such
Is my sense of your absence
That I keep myself neatly,
Completely
On my side of our bed?

Yet when I come in late, flushed, to find
The baby tucked in, house hushed,
Taps undripping,
Cats curled,
I ascend to bed and find you
Unfurled,
Your legs crossing borders,
Your arms unapologetically invading,
Body cascading right across
My side of our bed?

Beware those who read too much into too little...
And decipher discord in difference.

Big Boys Don't Cry

Grin and bear it,
Don't dare show it,
We all know Big Boys
Never cry.

Wound me verbally,
Strike me physically,
I'm here and I'm trying
To understand.

Show some emotion,
Don't go through the motions.
I love you. Please help me
To understand.

Sob and put it into words;
Bitter, screaming, spitting words.
Keep me in, throw out the world,
I will always understand.

Lean upon me as a brother,
Hold on to me as a mother,
I am here; I am your lover.
Do you understand?

Birthday Present

You told me: "It's OK, Mummy, you can go.
I can do it on my own;
You have taught me well."

My mouth smiled but, in my eyes, tears:
I glimpsed my death in years
To come.
Will you still
Say the same?

Your brother sat on the bottom step and whined
As little boys do, aged five—
Then bent and tied two skilful bows.

"Done, don't need you." Kissed me and left.
And though I was bereft,
I felt
The tide of pride;
I'd taught him well.

Blue-eyed Boy

Oh, my beautiful boy. There are some days,
Mamma's beloved blue-eyed boy...

I row my boat of joy through the ripples
On your lake of love;
I sun my face in the rays of your unselfconscious
Smile; I listen for giggles
Hidden in the lisping breeze,
Inhale the hidden corners of your neck
And twirl the dripping cone of your world
So we can lick the renegade "valinna" drops of life.
Each day you seek butterfly kisses from my eyelashes
Is a day of complete and utter love...

And there are other days, my beautiful boy...
Mamma's beloved blue-eyed boy...

When Peter-pointed fingers poke
Into unwoken eyeballs
And knees as sharp as yacht keels kneel to
Plough my tender tummy
While you, stern captain,
Issue harsh orders to "Wake up, mummy!"
So few days, my beautiful boy.
Each new day you grow and I learn
That loving you is a lesson in letting you go.

Oh, your days as my blue-eyed boy are too few.
More Mumma-days like *any* of these, please!
More days with my beloved blue-eyed boy.

Blue Tooth

Your blue-toothed head
Is perma-tuned to listen;
Yet you cannot hear me here.
You're ever-ready to speak,
Yet we cannot truly talk, converse:
You're averse to sitting eye-to-eye,
Toe-to-toe. It's just so
Impersonal. Fearful lest I touch/you touch me
Too much.
You'll blush infra-red
If I see you without that armour
On your head

Calliope's Drops

The washer's worn, but
For want of time I fail to replace
Wanton waste
With meaningful measures
Of fully filtered pints of poetry.
And yet, I find the dripping faucet strangely satisfying...
If I don't force it,
Can time the turning of the tap,
Keep baby, not bathwater,
And don't drop diamonds down the drain,
My masterpiece may yet be
In the pipeline.

Calliope is the ancient Greek muse of heroic poetry.

Cassius' Way

You've done that feline thing—
Padded in,
Found the warmest place,
Turned round three times
And claimed it as your space.

So clever of you to arrange
No change
To your own way of being—
Perhaps it's prismatic,
But that's what I'm seeing.

My possessions don't creep in when
You're sleeping.
Don't claim asylum on your shelves,
Economic refugees—
They keep themselves to themselves.

Perhaps I should try that feline thing?
Pad in,
Find your warmest place,
Turn round three times,
And claim it... But would you spare the space?

Cauldron

I slept, last night, on the rim
Of the cauldron of my
Children's dreams.

I woke, in fright, to a hymn,
To a murmured sweet cry,
To spells and schemes.

Awake, in the dark; full-brimmed
Their boiling dream-kettle sighed,
Hissed and screamed.

They woke, past dawn, bright-eyed,
Firmly rooted in daylight, sunshiny.
They kissed me, I yawned, and pried
Open eyes crusted with the briny
Overspill of childhood dreams.

Chakra Can

I stand
Wrapped in red:
Good fortune, Chinese-style.
It's hard to recognise order in your universe
When everything is out of place and nothing can get worse
And yet...

And yet,
Today I stand,
And scarlet visions say "I can".
I have come through it and survived.
Vermilion answers my sunlit thanks; wrapped in it, I thrive.
I'm touched...

I'm touched
That I've seen violet too.
Not feeling blue back then.
Was my third eye's message, "Change ahead,
Watch out"? I missed the signs and now I'm seeing red.
I wonder...

I wonder as I deconstruct the colour-code.
A celestial nod? Tipped a spiritual wink?
Is this chromatic message
An augury, or a reinforcement,
A question or an endorsement?
Who can say?

I can only say
My going-forward plan is to
Live a colourful life,
And always to believe I can.

ChildWoman

I'm spending my time just tilting at windmills.
A blind, Quixotic, frightened child,
Inside exotic, willful, wild,
Oppressed, repressed, recycled page.

I'm spending my time just gazing at scenery:
No-one believes that I do know what's right for me—
No-one can see the inside of me I can see.
"Child, things aren't like that, cannot and will never be."

Why does everyone take such pleasure in
Knocking the stilts from beneath my treehouse?
"See, little childwoman,
When all the props are gone,
Dreams cannot stop you from tumbling out."

Clowns' Tears

Cat Stevens already
Saw it more clearly.
But as I seek to follow more nearly
And love more dearly
I'm wondering if it's sad, or funny.

And so,
As I emerge,
Chrysalis-like,
From my confusion,
Have I actually reached any firm conclusion?

Am I
Any nearer
Feeling any clearer
About that elusive creature,
That amoebic concept, of "future"?

There are some
Things I know now,
Though many more I don't.
I've figured out some things I'll do before I die,
But, I'm pissed off about the thousand things I won't.

It's a journey
Of small increments.
Each step making a little more sense:
From improbable meetings with a wand-thin monk
(Teaching infinite consciousness, no colour, no shape)
From the "sod the lot of you" fear-filled funk,
To the thrill of possibility in the neck's bare nape...

So I'm rewarding myself with a minute's silence
To stop and listen to the still, small voice,
To the words that filter through the armour's chinks
In the moment when the heart stops pumping so the head
can think.

• Wonder

I'm rewarding myself with a minute's silence...
...
...
...

To follow more nearly
To love more dearly
To listen more clearly
To me.

Critique

The teacher-poet offered me his crisp critique:
"I like the way you fuck around with rhyme," he said.
And though it was sincerely meant, I'm sure,
As a compliment—
It offended me.

I went away and pondered his opinion;
I spent some time considering his views, his work, my
words.
And though I'm not at heart perverse, I'm sure,
I think his work is worse—
And that delighted me.

Debris

i am nobody, temporary insanity
plead it and you will see.
You don't know me, or owe me
no debt-collector, me.

i am week three of accumulated debris—
a dustman's strike
a passing fancy for a fattening pastry
you don't really like.

i am nobody, temporary insanity.
Leave it, walk away
walk away, leave it
walk
leave
away.
a passing fancy
debris.

Dungeness

I'm caught on the mesh at Dungeness.
Taken in.
If I could just ignore the
Nuclear next-door
I could relax,
And slip like a sprat back into circulation
Through the pebbledash of tides.

But I (like a blank-eyed cottage
Or abandoned boat),
Stay and stare out to sea,
To see
What it's all about.
But I doubt if anything's worth this energy.

Easy Like a Sunday Morning

Static-free, her silken underwear (soft peaches)
Falls to the polished parquet, her converted warehouse floor.
Phone rings and from her scented bath she reaches,
While downstairs—tall and handsome—he leaves roses at
her
door.

Freshly washed, her silken tresses (honey blonde)
Fall to her sculpted shoulders (Azzedine Alaïa-clad).
In her car, purrs down the gravel drive, beyond
Which waits his bachelor's oak-paneled country pad.

Lean, cuisine, soft candlelight and filter coffee:
Special blend, in boxer shorts, the real man unties his bow.
A Courtney Pine CD, pine bed and toffee satin
Sheets: condom on, his dimmer turns the lights down low.

On his gabled window, stark white wooden shutters
Split the trembling moonlight shining on his Rolex face.
His mongrel whines, a single scented candle gutters
The dog paws at the woman's poignant, empty space...

Where has she gone? How could she leave this heaven?
This life of Fifties fridges, low-fat yoghurt, modern art.
Had she counted down the years and got to seven
Couldn't live a moment longer in an ad, afraid to fart?

Eight Mile

I get the rap,
But where's the *rapture*?
Can you capture
The gentle,
The sentimental?
Or is it lost in the neuralgia
Of drugs
The myalgia of thugs
Landing punches;
Bunches of knuckles,
Not nasturtiums.
Truculent hours
In basements
Mouthing profanity
Into a mixing desk
That channels inanity.
Where is the beauty?
Where the Lily?
Can you gild the rhymes you build?

"Eight Mile" is the title of a film starring (and based on the early life of) rap music star, Eminem.

• Wonder

Elsewhere

It was night-time.
I lay on my back between twisted sheets
And gazed out of the uncurtained window
At a blue haze
Whose deepest edges
Were misted gold
With light from the scattered streetlamps.

Without my noticing
My mind stepped quietly through a hole
In the sky
And I found myself...

Elsewhere.
These are the whimpers and twitches.
These are the hours of voodoo kings,
Of sprites, imps, druids and witches.

No new messages.
I saw before me a vast valley, a chasm
Between pages, on which were written
The lessons of
The previous decade.
Could I, I wondered
Ignore them and search for another truth...

Elsewhere?
These are the whimpers and twitches.
The petty irritations, minor triumphs,
The wriggles and niggles and itches.

Everything He's Not

He sits, secure in his white middle age,
(His special pencils sharpened),
Pausing before his hand-made page,
Waiting, not daring to engage.

Unable to forget himself, even momentarily,
(Prowess murmurs from the mantle),
He recalls a boyhood episode, but warily,
As the bog of reputation slurps so scarily.

Some light adventure in a country school
(Pleasing prank, readily accessible).
Make certain he's not cast as fool...
So market forces guide his genius-tool.

A self-conscious yester-was seeking rewards—
(Gold in any guise inspires);
The scratch of nib and sniff of new awards
Mark out the path to rewrite and reword.

A stuffed shirt, decaying: can't you smell it?
(Monogrammed, no stain of sweat.)
Why fight to write when those initials sell it?
Hand in hand, the dollars dance and quell it.

Rest in peace, painful truth, we need not know it:
For here writes a popular and successful poet.

---

*A tribute to Seamus Heaney, whom I had the privilege to meet
and read with at the 2006 Man Hong Kong International Literary
Festival.*

Familiarity

You see me most clearly
Reflected in the eyes of the
Foundlings I flirt with.

Skipping nimbly round the rim
Of our social circle
I weave webs of wine and wonder,
Scatter sparkles into others' lives.

And yet, at home,
Looking into my eyes,
What can you find to say, except,
"Familiarity breeds contempt."

Feltham Youth Custody Centre: 6am

Bars—with birds outside them,
Heading south to where it's warm.
You wake up and it's snowing—
Hate those birds: you won't be going.

The bed's so hard your back's in pain,
The snow is warming into rain.
Each day inside tightens the screw—
There's nothing to look forward to:

Doors that slam, and locks and keys,
The reptile house and night's unease,
Lock-up, lock-down, bland beige food;
Nothing to relieve the mood.

So, it's time to wake up,
Time to get up,
Time to shave.
Emotions,
Motions,
Automatic,
Life as routine's slave:
Prepare yourself for kit inspection...
No time to indulge in introspection.

We come in here with our college smiles,
Filling in forms for a couple of miles;
Stay just long enough for you to miss us,
Want us, need us, dream of kisses.

Back in the "real world", we'll discuss you,
Analyse and think we've sussed you.
Talk of hardship, have a moan,
Stifle our superior groans.

• Wonder

While boy-man in his cell writes poems
(Most he'd never think of showing);
Condenses his world in a scribbled gem:
What's the difference, me and them?

While studying law I was part of a drama group called Project YCC. We stayed for several weekends each year in youth custody centres, creating shows with the inmates. One year I worked in the psychiatric unit (nicknamed the reptile house) and discovered a wonderful young poet.

Fickle boy

Where has my muse gone?
I'm deserted.

Is he living, debauched, in some London mews,
An amused pout on his fickle lips,
Taking sips of some other's summer wine,
Twining words into thick coils of useful rhyme,
Tracing fingertip filigree up the supine spine

Of some dreaming poet
Other than me?
Well, is he?

Final

There are days when I wake and wonder.
As, once again, with steely purpose,
I shackle study to wrist and ankle,
I wonder.

There are evening sunsets that glow and I wonder.
As gaily-painted people gad,
And leave me tied to my angle-poise,
I wonder.

First Change

At my body's first change
I stretched my sweaters long at sleeve and hem
To hide my metamorphosis
From the you I viewed as "them".

No butterfly, I.
Emerged too earthy, made of big bones and solid olive skin.
And now, lived in for many decades,
It's a boon to shed the cocoon

As change begins anew.
As I become an old me, I wear my clothing boldly
To show you—and them—
My metamorphosis is not yet complete.

Fragments

On the outside
I'm a big girl
Dreaming of a little adventure.

On the inside
I'm a little girl
Dreaming of a big adventure.

* * *

The way you disparage me
Begins to discourage me.
When you belittle my big heart
You belie your own.

* * *

It's a near miss,
We're so near bliss,
Can we sort this out?

We're halfway
Down the pathway
To a lifelong love.

Friendship

... And so I ring you, and we chat.

"How's the baby? D'you fancy dinner?
I saw her today and she's looking thinner.

He's working too hard. We need a break.
I bought it in the market. No, it's not a fake!

Then what'd you say? Good for you!
She's really not a patch on you.

I *like* your hair. What time does it start?
I tried a spanner, but it's missing a part.

I'm feeling great. When can we meet?
Really? Why not? But that's next week!

I'm really fed up, and feeling flat..."
... And so I ring you, and we chat.

For ER.

Genocide

Our world has watched its loveliness raped, and buried
In a shallow grave to putrefy; humanity has been
Trodden underfoot and trampled.

Brains blown out by babies serving hate-gods or partisan
politics;
Advised by square-jawed, sure-fired monsters...
Frankenstein lives and is uncontrollable.

A shield, a glow of self-satisfied certainty will insulate us
every morning,
Will vaccinate us against the plague of slime insinuating,
Incinerating flesh.

You and I, we need not see how close we come to death:
We cannot feel the gun against our temple, taste the
mettle
Of our bleeding.

Hatred beyond all understanding poses itself—a solid black
silhouette
With eyes of arson—at the top of every ridge, and pitches
Humiliated corpses headlong over till they
Pile and lose all meaning.

Honour and dignity in death become unreal, untouchable,
When the dignity of life means nothing more than spit
... And blood
... And dirt
... And ignorance.

Golden Opportunity

My life-days have lost an essential beauty,
Enmeshed and ensnared by deadline and duty.
While cathedral stones tincture pink in the morning,
I tread a grey carpet, reality dawning;
In unorthodox uniform—uniformed still
I churn out my paper, the grist to their mill.

***

We throw the bruised and battered baby bushes in the bin,
And breathe the pre-conditioned air that suffocates the skin.
We run after-work excursions with a stifled spontaneity...
To bed, in time to rise again and praise the dollar deity.

***

"There are no problems, only opportunities":
You blinked and missed it (ladder turned to snake).
For forty years, climb up from where you started
And try to cling on when the ladder shakes.

***

We grasp the golden grains of weekend.
Sands of time through fingers floorwards sift.
We gaze in wonder (falling sand's so pretty) —
No time to stand and watch the sand dunes drift.

***

The world changed shape while I was in the office:
Clouds furled, spread and babies drew first breath;
Art was revolutionised and somewhere,
Somebody put someone else to death.

***

But me, I was too busy pushing paper,
And sitting on a fence in rosy specs.
My terms of reference insulate,
My food and learning isolate...
My ivory tower inviolate.

Guardian Angel

I struggle to seek help or
Accept assistance,
I choose the path of most resistance;
Yet you,
You are my guardian angel.

I deny myself shelter in
The harshest storm,
You wrap arms around me, so I'm dry and warm,
Because you,
You are my guardian angel.

You found me.
You ground me.
You keep me.
You seek me...
You even forgive me:
The strong and the weak me.
I thank you,
My guardian angel.

Hip, Hip, Eurasia

Banker with lots of body hair and limited imagination,
With big wallet and little concentration
Seeks
Local woman with small breasts and big lips,
With clear needs and slim hips
For
Perfect cross-cultural communication.
(Less social intercourse than financial miscegenation,
For
Life, side-by-side without intersection,
Is his monolingual aspiration).
Yet
Their offspring are universally spectacular,
Confluent in occidental and oriental vernacular...
So there's high hope for our Eurasian future.

How to be a Domestic Goddess

I scorched the recipe.
You see,
The irony's not lost on me.

The gas ring's
Branded
On the cover. My lover

Says the truth
I seek
Lies at the tip of the tongue lodged firmly in his cheek.

"How to Be a Domestic Goddess" is the title of a Nigella Lawson recipe book. I left my copy on top of the hot cooker and burned the cover, to the amusement of my husband, an artist in the kitchen.

Hurt

The brow I kiss crinkles
With sadness? Or pain?
The heart in me twists
Till I've smoothed it again.

Lips I love so, compress
Till the feeling subsides.
Legs I've often caressed
Shake the hurt from inside.

That body that's come
To mean so much to me,
Feels a pain I can't help
From a hurt I can't see.

How I'd love just to kiss
All sensations away
Except for those you and I
Both want to stay.

I Believe in the Possibility That Life Can Happen...

Did gigantic Jupiter protect the Earth;
Deflect cometary impact?
Where were the planets at the moment of your birth,
Where on Earth?

We are all stars: particles of moon shattered in some
                                        ancient collision.
But it's not astronomical intervention
That defines our search for civilization.
We feel intelligent beings must inhabit other stars;
Our intelligence (artificial), creates stars on television
Thrives on negative media attention;
Sows the seeds of our own destruction.

If our planet's turning on its axis, is that a scientific
                                        revolution?
We need to apply some creative imagination:
"A rock won't answer unless you ask it a question."
You're smart; understand that genius ain't science.
It pulls the sleeves of thought seam-side out, dream-side out,
It sows the seeds of doubt
Finds truffles with its snotty snout...

Did gigantic Jupiter protect the Earth;
Deflect cometary impact?
Where were the planets at the moment of your birth,
Where on Earth?

The wonderful Margaret Atwood appeared at the 2009 Man Hong Kong International Literary Festival. This piece was inspired by her presentation to students: funny, erudite, earthy and scientific.

ImPerfect

Who wouldyoucouldyoushouldyou have been
If not the you you are?
And if you were that other you,
Wouldweshouldwecouldwe love you more?

Can we make you the you in our mind's eye?
Wouldwecouldweshouldwe even try?
Tell me, are we so blind we cannot see
Beyond the you you might have been?

Couldweshouldwewouldwe ever accept the truly you,
(The you that you will live your life to be)?
Wouldyoushouldyoucouldyou please help us accept you
And everything you wearerewillbe?

For my nephew, WDT, whose premature birth resulted in brain haemorrhage, cerebral palsy and blindness. He has oceans of patience, a wicked sense of humour and a huge hug capacity.

• Wonder

Intensive Care

Look at you now, Mr Yellow-Belly
Cowardy-Custard.
Jaundiced eyes see
You could never cut the mustard
You old bastard.
Porcupined
With fourteen kinds of needle.
Not an optic in sight,
Ironically, and yet with every drip
You lose your grip on me and I
Let rip...

You did this to yourself!
You did this to yourself,
You selfish old git.
And we're all here for you,
Again. More pain, no gain,
Just the same:
Trying to come to terms with your shit.

How does it feel? Are you scared?
Is it worse than you faced
Every morning
Pouring scotch on Cornflakes?
You old bastard.
Abused
By all these tubes full of misery
You're suddenly shy.
Here with your family
You waste your lucidity on cheap cruelty:
"What are you here for? Waiting for me to die?"

You did this to yourself!
You did this to yourself,
You selfish old git.
And we're all here for you,
Again. More pain, no gain,
Just the same:
Trying to come to terms with your shit.

Look at you now, you chickenshit.
Too sedated for shame
So you'll let it end
With nothing more than more of the same—
You old bastard.
Death like life:
Your children and wife merit
No attention.
Ironically, the Landlord's calling time
And I'm left angrily watching you lose your grip and I
Let rip...

You did this to yourself!
You did this to yourself,
You selfish old git.
And we're all here for you,
Again. More pain, no gain,
Just the same:
Trying to come to terms with your shit.

For L, D & P.

• Wonder

International School for Scandal

Look at those teenage goddesses,
So gorgeously gauche.
Attributes
Without attitude:
Blossoming blowjob lips,
Slender, swinging hips,
Nails with fresh French tips...
And no clue how to use them.

Look at those pubescent portraits,
So pointedly pouting;
Painted,
But unsigned.
Posed expressions,
Shaping so many questions,
Offering so few suggestions.
Utterly unsure what their body's for.

There ought to be a law
Against youthful inexperience
And the gravity of age.

Lady Living in a Foreign Land

She's fifty,
And the ground has started to shift, she
Is feeling cast adrift; see
Her children sail for new beginnings
On old shores.

The doors close,
And all the questions her life's posed
Begin to gather like shadows.
She's seeking answers she hasn't found...
And time ticks on.

The worst part
Is splitting a hard head from a soft heart,
For living a real life is a fine art.
The money trap's sprung and is
Liberally baited.

Yet the lure
Of the lyre and the lyric lingers
And the devil makes work for indolent fingers...
She's searching for the thing worth doing well, and
There's one... last... chance.

For CWG.

Larger Than Life

He was a big man,
Square of head and round of bottom,
Once met, not easily forgotten.

He had a huge heart:
He built a world of love around the world
Founded on his wife and little girls.

He was a fine husband—
A friend and comrade, a constant lover.
Fine father. Fine son. Fine Grandpa, uncle, brother.

He loved to gather knowledge,
To store and retrieve all sorts of information,
Discuss, digest, dissect it and—always—pass it on.

His were strong hands.
He had an artist's eye and a craftsman's sense:
He loved to touch, to make and mend.

His was a wicked sense of humour.
He loved a good story, bawdy, a splash of sauce,
To tease, to talk and to laugh, of course.

His was a Grandpa's indulgence:
Endless songs and stories, a way with words —
For parenthood, grandchildren were his reward.

His was a death under a rainbow, and
Though we can only feel the rain now,
He knew the sun had started shining...
That's why he fought so hard to stay.

He was a man much-loved.
His was a life well-lived.
His full heart overflowed.
Life was his final gift.

Last Day of Summer

I am Mother Earth, gesturing defiance at winter.
I am the single swallow that makes a summer.
I am dawn's bucketful of Indian sunshine.
I am the child of the last day of summer.

I am the laughter lines cracking in baked earth.
I am the burning sand's squeal underfoot.
I am the bareness appearing, a rebirth.
I am the child of the last day of summer.

I am the castles each man may storm.
I am the phosphorescent bodies at night.
I am the seducer, inducing undress,
I am the child of the last day of summer.

Banished by winter, I flee into night.
Stealthy, in dreams, I sketch scenes of delight,
Till, day-by-day, willed by warm hearts I take flight...
And alight each year, Child of the last day of light.

Like a Mad Thing

"Well, if you will run round like a mad thing,
you must expect to fall down sometimes."
The logic is sound,
But the magic is missing.

"You've got your head in the clouds half the time,
so of course you trip and tumble."
I slip and stumble,
But I've kissed the sun.

"You're off with the fairies all day long. No wonder the real
world scares you."
How dare you presume
To know my fears.

I reach beyond for
The things I long for.
I try to fly because
We've all got to die
Someday.
I risk the pain to
Make my mundane
Extraordinary,
To create a plot
For my life story.

Love Ltd

Mother with her baby in a sling
Pushes through the big, glass corporate door
And lets it swing
Shut
On the pushchair of another mother's baby.
Now,
Maybe that glass conceals
A reason,
But to me it reveals
Small minds
Living in limited love.
And, surely,
Life should be for
Collaboration, not competition.

Little Bird

I

Time to fly free, little bird.
Away from the trunk-wide span of his body,
Away from the branch-like breadth of his arms,
Away from the hand that slaps with the crack
Of chestnut limbs whipped by a hurricane wind.

Time to break free, little bird.
You've shaken your tail feathers bravely,
You've hatched your brood in your well-feathered nest,
You've sung and danced under fury-fuelled fists
Spreading shame and blame and bruises.

Time to fly free, little bird.
Away from the "what-did-I-do?" self-doubt,
Away from the "what-did-I-say?" salt tears,
Away from the father who broke your flesh and your heart
But not your will... And where there's a will, there's away.

II

I hate you, Dad; I love you
You hate me, Dad; I love you
You shame me, Dad; I love you
I blame me, Dad; I love you.

III

Strong arms round a little baby,
Strong hands pound a little girl,
Strong words hound a grieving woman
Strong hearts break as you leave this world.

IV

Tell me...

What did I do, Daddy?
Why did you hate me?
What did I say, Daddy?
Why did you hit me?
How can I change, Daddy,
So you can love me?
How should I be, Daddy,
So you won't hurt me?

Now I am grown, Daddy,
Grown with a baby.
I've tried to be you, Daddy,
But I think maybe
That's my mistake.
I've been letting you take
What is me. I'm *not* you.
So now what do I do?

You can't speak or explain,
So I'm left with this pain.
I'm adrift and bereft,
Picking up what is left;
With a question for you,
"Tell me, what did I do?"...
Though I know it was you—all you.

Every blow I lived through,
It was all about *you*.
Do you know what has struck me?
I was just a baby.
It was you,
It was all about you...
So why do I ask,
"Daddy, what did *I* do?"

V

You were always my number one.
Me, your third—neither firstborn nor son.
Me, your third—the unwanted one.

Remember me? I look like you.
My words, my ways, they're like you too.
But I love my child, unlike you.

I learned your lessons, every one.
I will not teach them to my son,
For he's my beloved, my number one.

VI

I like to look at adverts for life insurance.
I like the love, the easy self-assurance
Of those colour-poster characters.

I gaze at the dads who toss their bonny babies
Up into a sunlit world of so few maybes
And always, *always* catch them.

For LGL.

• Wonder

Love Letterbox

Grandma had her bosom cut off 'cause there was cancer in it.
I saw the scar and said, "It looks like a letterbox."

Grandma said if I posted enough love into her heart every day
Maybe it would grow into a nice new bosom one day.

So every morning I gave Grandma a great, big cuddle
And pressed my love up against her chest.

Grandma had radiotherapy. That's not like dancing to music;
Your hair doesn't fall out dancing. I couldn't stick it back.

Grandma said stroking her head makes her hair grow quicker.
So I touched all the bald bits and wished for curls.

Grandma says the doctor drew on her and took photos inside.
I photographed her pirate scarf and jellyfish-bosom swimsuit.

Grandma took tablets that were all the rainbow colours.
"Do they taste happy?" I asked. "No, they taste like thunder."

Grandma had to lie down because she was feeling sick,
So I spooned behind her and told her my roses from school.

Grandma got a brand new bosom two weeks ago.
No letterbox, no cancer. So now I just put ordinary love on my Lips and kiss her anyway.

For MED.

Ma & Pa

"They fuck you up…"

Mine never did.
My nicks and cuts
Healed up.
I've no scars hid.

They just love you.
Mine do—
And always did.

The opening line is a quotation from Philip Larkin's poem, 'This Be the Verse'.

Martyr

Living on eggshells:
Permanently perspiring,
No-one demanding,
Just simply requiring solicitude.

Dancing on ashes:
Tiptoes or tantrums,
Nobody smiling—
No wind through the doldrums of crisis.

Burying hatchets:
Embed them in warm hearts;
Unseen, six foot under,
We bleed from the soft parts we're hiding.

Wilderness winter:
Disdaining, despairing,
Invisible mending:
Papered cracks, or repairing existence?

Mid-Life Cry

Sis!
Big sis, little sis,
Your advice:
What should I do about this mid-life cry?
Sis, I'm 44,
Double death,
One year of breaths
Closer, I'm certain, to
The closing curtain.

For CJK & ELD.

• Wonder

Miriam, the Welsh Dragon

Angry and irascible to the last day,
She went to sleep and passed away.

"You're good," she pointed, and still she glared.
Which meant, "Of course I always cared."

And with that, and a pat on the hand,
Went to her Maker at peace with Ann.

"What on Earth are you doing *now*?"
To the doctor; to the nurse, an old cow.

Pulling out tubes. What an iron will:
Ninetieth year, and so rarely ill.

But she'd seen our fourth generation twice,
There was nothing more she wanted from life.

Wherever she's gone, there'll be plenty waiting:
A husband and siblings she'll already be baiting.

And true to our history, our clan was abroad.
Better, perhaps; we're so noisy a horde.

And she'll come back, I know, with some things she must
                                        menti
                        on
Like, "Why are you scruffy?", "Have you set up your
pension?"

She loved us in ways that were complicated....
I was due home so soon, I just wish she had waited.

For MJ.

Mottled

Poetry. For me its principal function is honesty.
Hard thoughts softened by beautiful constructs;
Sweet sounds wrapped round pain.

So I choose to write about marble-mottled markings
On flesh no longer fresh. Where oceanic blood flows.
Blue-green traces mark the places where new life took its
toll.

Alone, I take myself in, wholeheartedly,
Markedly distasteful, the map I lay bare:
Tracks, roads and intersections
Mar my former golden grasslands.

• Wonder

Negative Space

Strange how, if we only learn to look,
The shadows show us where the light is shining.

Funny that the same measure of a grave
Marks the length of a life, however it was lived.

Now that form following function
Has failed to reveal my clouds' silver lining,

It's time to become more brave
And carve my rock using all the tools I have to hand.

A blinding ray of light, a thunderbolt,
Would be fine, of course, but I'll smile and settle

For a soft glow where my next foot
Should fall, on the path that will test my mettle.

OutLoud

I love to hear poetry read aloud.

I love the voyeuristic peep
Into the recesses deep in the writer's mind;
The literary glimpse into their bathroom cabinet,
The drawer beside their bed,
The intimate rummage inside a poet's head.

I love the frisson from
Half-seen nakedness, the obtuse openness
Of a curious mind above a mouth full of secrets;
A poet's full-moon arse
Glimpsed through frosted glass.

We poets wiggle our selves like bait for Fate.
Disguised as artistic purity
Our vanity and insecurity lure them in
And we lie in wait for the bite of Wednesday night...
When we stand to read our poetry OutLoud.

Renaissance Man

Have you ever seen it?
It's called a cartoon,
But it's not funny.

It's da Vinci's drawing of a helicopter.

Before they fully understood
The planet's crazy revolutions
He invented it.

It's da Vinci's drawing of a helicopter.

He was so clever
(I'd love to meet him)
But he forgot: "Danger, Stand Back!"

It's da Vinci's drawing of a helicopter.

It kicks up dust,
Blinds you to the obvious
And chops you to pieces.

It's da Vinci's drawing of a helicopter.

The blades are held on by
Just one nut: the Jesus nut.
Without it, all hell breaks loose.

It's da Vinci's drawing of a helicopter.

Leonardo da Vinci created conceptual drawings (dated 1483) of a device that anticipated a modern helicopter. The Jesus nut is the castellated nut that secures the rotors on a helicopter.

Road Rage

The roads are cluttered with nutters whose utter
Contempt for the rules makes fools
Of those who drive alongside.

They drive as if lives are cheap. Won't lose sleep;
The blood spattered won't matter
If they get where they're going.

But surely it's not about fast and first,
It's all about home and whole?

Ruminatin'

So, if I give a yak curls
Like a black girl's
Then it turns twirls
Did I create an afro dizzy yak?

Sand

And so, my firstborn child,
I give you the gift of sand.
Sands of time
Mined from the mountain of moments
That used to be mine.

Time for people, places and purposes you love;
Time to find patience and fortitude to face
All that seeks to grind you down
To sand.

Beautiful, beautiful child
Just as every grain of sand is itself, perfectly,
So I love you—for being
So perfectly you.

And just as sand is the sum
Of many grains, you are destined for life in a wide world:
Respect other lives, for each—like yours—
Is unique.

Stone, shell and coral.
Once here and whole. Now parts of the dream castles
Built by babies in the air, or on
Sea-washed shores.

And so, firstborn child of mine,
Delightful, devastating daughter—
My reward and my retribution—
Receive the sands of my time.

This gift I give you knowing that it can never be enough—
And yet, it must be. For when my time runs out,
Our glittering moments must become the rock
On which your life is built:

• Wonder

Solid,
Strong,
Yet ready to become
The gift of sand
For your firstborn child.

For ECL.

Self-Satisfied

You crave the disapproval
Of those you despise;
You court their condemnation.

You peel back the layers
Of comfortable lies
For closer examination.

And those whose foibles
You scrutinize
Resent their evisceration.

You crave the disapproval
Of those you despise;
You court their condemnation.

For PJL.

So Long

You've been
So good
For
So long,
So how
Did this happen?

I'm asking
Why now
And
Why you?
Why not
Play it safe?

You tell me
What's new
And
What's you...
But is "What's next?"
The question?

Stand To

Mr E. "It-stands-to" Reason
Has two rheumy, washed-blue eyes,
And his pinstriped, paper-bag-like suit
Holds a story twice his size.

"I'm an insurance consultant,
But I fought in World War Two.
I biked through France to reach Bordeaux,
Jumped on a boat to bring me home,
Volunteered to join the Gunners,
Then transferred to the Int Corps runners.
I was in for the duration,
Fighting in the desert stations;
Quite fun, really, between the killing—
Not like the trenches, bloody and swilling—
Lots of sunshine, I learned Egyptian..."
He's a living, dying work of fiction.
"Made it home to my wife and raised my son...
Well, you know... Life just goes on."

Mr E. "It-stands-to" Reason
Has two rheumy, washed-blue eyes,
And his pinstriped paper-bag-like suit
Holds a story twice his size.

In 1988, in an old people's home in Toronto, Canada, I met some men who had fought in the Second World War, and a few who had fought in both world wars. I treasure memories of my time spent with their gas-rattle voices, holding 108-year old hands, and the humble humour of Mr Reason, a truly heroic gentleman. "Int Corps" refers to the British Army's Intelligence Corps.

Still Hazy

Hey bro'
Wha's happenin'?
What, no hello?
What's eatin' you?
No, I *don't* know —
I'm still hazy after all these beers.

Say what?
Say I said you have a shallow life?
Say I stabbed your heart and twisted the knife?
Did I *say* I didn't like your wife?
Well, I don't remember, bro'...
I'm still hazy after all these beers.

Did I say you're the anti-Christ! Blasphemy?
That hatin' talk, that just ain't me!
Dissin' you? Man, you dissin' me!
Dis ain't the way it was meant to be, bro'.

Bro'? Man?

Talk to me, man. I miss you. I love you.
Where are you? Did *she* make you go there?
I feel like I've lost you. I need a sign.
Where'd you go? How can I find you?
Bro', come back, you're mine.

No? No? But bro'...

Well, then, can I meet you halfway?
But you'll have to give me directions, man,
I mean, I don't know the world you live in.
I ain't been where you been or seen what you seen, man
And, well, I'm kind of ashamed to admit it, but I guess I'm
still A little hazy after all these beers.

Stillness

I ploughed twenty-three years of my life
Into the fields of your existence,
And made them fertile with our children.

I built homes out of the houses,
Papered the walls with love,
Cried tears into the paintwork.

And now it's... almost...
A relief that you've gone.

For AS.

• Wonder

Strange Parlay

Your frail birth—so fortunate.
For though your fitting fist
Drummed on the door of death
Your newborn knuckles knocked too soft.
Your arm, protesting, raised aloft,
Went unremarked by he who chooses
Who embarks to sail across by ferry.

The very idea of you leaving
Set us grieving. Our wails
Rent holes in the sails
And strange parlay began,
Trading boy for man:
An I for an eye, or two.
And who are we to call our bargains
Anything but God's gift to the Future?

Telethon

I'm sorry, Madam,
We've had a rush on
Cheap compassion.

I don't have anything in your size,
Small hearts aren't in this season,
That's the reason.

I've some things in green, but they wouldn't suit
Your (political) complexion.
That's no reflection on you, of course.

Fundraisers?
Yes, we do fund razors
And bandages, blankets, tents and soup.

Your scoop-necked Gucci with the satin ribbon binding...?
I might have trouble finding
A refugee to fit it...
You're generous in the waste (no pun intended)
If not the spirit.

Two Women

They stand,
These two women,
On the rim of the waves,
Allowing their feet to sink, softly, into each sandy onrush
                                                    and
Hushed retreat.

They watch,
Two fond friends,
What their children build,
As the swirling waves mark not high water, but a circle of
                                                    love
'Round their feet.

They talk—
Two ageing women—
Easily, deeply and truly,
About the laughter, the love, the loss and the learning in
                                                    the
Shared lives they've known.

One day,
Other women,
Newer to this sand, will stand
In their footprints; laugh, and cry, and talk—for two
                                                    women
Together are never alone.

For KBF

LUST

"The sentiment is excessive, blowsy, loose, womanish. But I am willing to blurt it all out, if only to myself. Blurting is a form of bravery. I'm just catching on to that fact."

—Carol Shields
Unless

• Lust

A Wife's Life

"I just want my life back
For a while,"
She said.
He tried to smile
But didn't make it—
Just a bit too hard to fake it—
So he cried
And died a little
Inside
Instead.

Affairs of the Heart

I'm thinking of having an affair.
There,
It's said.
The bed of another man beckons
And the day of reckoning will come.

I'm dreaming of a lover's touch;
So much
More exciting
Than a husband's hold,
So old, and well-established.

• Lust

Beautiful Day

I wake to your kisses
Measuring the breadth of my back.

I wake to the warmth
Of a sun-filled, lavender sky.

I wake, and my mind's eye
Is filled with the promise

Of a beautiful day.

Betrayal

She imagines the detailed scenario.
Traces fingertips
Across his lips

And feels the shape of possibility.
Her mouth's on
Expedition south

As she brailles trails over every inch.
But she's clutching
A fistful of wistful.

Between the Sheets

Nobody else knows.

Nobody else knows what goes on
Between the sheets.

Between the sheets of our story.
Sheets of vellum, papyrus, of fish wrap.

Bound with gum and thread and love.
Bound into our autobiography.

Nobody else knows what goes on
Between the sheets.

Creamy Filling

My favourites are the ones with soft centres.
With a creamy filling.

The ones that make you lick your lips before you bite
That melt—oh, so willing.

And after—make you lick your lips again.
Not chocolates, darling...

Men!

Dissolution

An old love letter,
A half-empty cup of cooling coffee
Still faintly warm,
Ringed round
With old stains,
Crumpled crisp packets:
The debris of human storms.

So much ceremony
Reduced to so little.
A decree
Signed in silence:
The sound of fanfares
Faded into inkblots.

It's so sad.
I'm so sad...
And sorry.

For SP.

Doormat

You treat me like a door, Matt:
You enter me
Then leave me,
Bang me,
And walk away.

Heaven on Earth

For what it's worth,
That's what it was about:
Getting a longer stretch
Of Heaven on Earth.

Pushing my luck.
That's what I was up to—
Looking to be more lucky me.
No passing the buck.

Fate sometimes stretches
A bit further at no extra cost,
But sometimes the whole game's lost
And she leaves you wretched.

I know how it's been isn't *real*.
For what it's worth
It's been Heaven on Earth,
How you made me feel.

But I pushed my luck
And fucked it
Up.

Hot as Wasabi

I want you to mix wasabi
And soy sauce in my belly button,
And eat sushi from the pliable plate of my flesh;
To lap and chew and sup
From me—your moveable feast.

How the Email Killed the He-Man

I used to dream of plumbers:
Burly body sporting wrench,
Unscrewing every U-bend
For this "Help me! Save me!" wench.

Some nights, cops got a look-in—
I quite like a boy in blue.
Movies weren't a source of fantasy:
My he-men need a use.

But lately it's been glasses—
Not men fitting window panes—
I dream no more of biceps,
I'm fixated on boys' brains.

Since I bought my brand-new laptop
All my dreams have gone awry.
Before that I was not turned on
By intellectual guys.

But this dreamboat's flying fingers
Touching all those plastic keys
Seem to press my bed-time buttons
With a quiet, insouciant ease.

In the prior years, a "turn on"
Hadn't such a literal sense,
But those little lights start flashing,
And my power surge's immense.

And when we come to download,
Well, it's quite unlike before,
And every time we backslash,
Well, it all feels quite hardcore.

So my bloke dreams are all over,
Not replaced by someone chic;
My bedtime fantasy partner's
Morphed from plumber into geek.

• Lust

Interstitial Spaces

That's where silence reigns,
where we rein in galloping hearts and
saying nothing, move apart.

The interstitial spaces are the quiet overflowing places
where whirlpools gather, where words are reabsorbed
like mistimed babies; where full-felt feelings fade,
unused, unspoken,
unformed,
so hearts and vows, like mother's best cupboard-kept
teacups, remain
unbroken.

Here we're defined, spined, book-ended
by silent proper nouns and breathy sibilants
sighed over paper skin.

The interstitial spaces mark the transition between
                                                    places;
where the I and me almost meet with the he and she;
where the never ever "we" resides in homely comfort free
of shame.
Unwelcome,
Madonna, Magdalen and Me; like panels of a triptych,
we're separate; like altar candles,
in flames.

Laughing All the Way to the Bank

When our fortunes are told,
We'll hold the predictions in the palms of our hands,
Deft, like lace
Patterning its weft through my fingertips' sweet filligree
On your face.

Your fortune's in the making.
You're taking pains as you cross my path and my heart,
Like a snail,
Not to cross my palm with silver, lest you leave a shining
Traceable trail.

All the truths your silent-spiralled shell conceals might
Come to light, tonight.

The half-truths in the half-light
Look us in the eye, give a painful poke to all the words
On which we choke.
We blink instead; nothing to say, your silver tongue and
Dollars turned to lead.

My head on your treasure(d) chest.
I wrote, in dregs and dusty lees from the bottle you left
Me nursing.
The casual effrontery of your silence in front of me
Left me cursing.

All the truths your silent-spiralled shell conceals might
Come to light, tonight.

This time, next time, last time...
The penny (gold or silver, good or bad) drops like a
Rotten apple,
For such is the gravity of the situation with which
We grapple.

Layer Cake—And Eat It

We're a layer of complication
That neither of us wants or needs;
We're too old and tired to rummage more
In this package of misdeeds.

I'm a bundle of contradictions
And it's too hard to sort it out.
Is it lifelong impossible to be content
Doing what's clearly thought out?

We're colliding parallel universes
A comedic pile-up of if-onlys.
Lying bruised and scattered kerb-side:
We both deserve to be lonely.

How much better could it get, you ask?
How bad could it really be?
Surrounded by so much perfection
We mope that "it's not about me".

Stand up, stand up, like a Kipling man!
And dance like a Ziegfeld girl;
Your follies are human, your hearts divine,
And your costume's all atwirl.

If you shift your focus outwards
There are eyes that are focused on you
And they're all watching closely to find out
What exactly you will do.

So kiss and make up, share a handshake
Because that is how good friends behave,
And then play back the game in slow motion:
You won with a lucky save.

Yes, that surely would be the smart choice,
That would be the way of the wise,
But there's fool's gold out in them there hills
And the search is the real prize.

It's the sugar-coated moment
(Though the thing itself's half-baked)
That makes life worth the living,
That ices the layers of cake.

The fifth stanza quotes from the poem, 'The English Way' by
Rudyard Kipling. It also alludes to the "Ziegfeld Follies",
Broadway shows launched in 1907 whose dancers were reputed
to be the most beautiful girls in the world.

• Lust

Leap

Look
Before you love
Before you cross the road
After yourself.

Don't look
Into the sun
Under the lavatory door
So smug.

Find
What you're looking for
Out about your history
A soulmate.

Ask
For help
For a hand in marriage
Me.

Love Among the Greenwoods

You are my heart of oak:
Rooted in native England,
Canopy spread wide.
Acorns dropped far from the tree
Now grow their own sweet shade.

Mighty, your heart of oak,
Seasoned by wind and weather.
The tall roof beam shakes,
Cracked by time; the barn remains,
While we make foreign hay.

A traditional British barn is built from green (unseasoned) oak. As the wood ages and dries out, it moves slightly, creating natural cracks (known as "shakes") in the timber.

Man and Wife

I prowl your cupboards
Seeking signs of you:
Indications,
Weigh stations,
Explanations.

In another life,
At a different crossroads,
With a tilt of the compass,
Am I your wife?

My scent's on your pillows—
An unkind thing to do.
Past's extinct,
Choice distinct,
Animal instinct.

What kind of story
Would our tell-tale tale tell?
Adventure or misadventure,
Death or glory?

If I violate both our vows
I abuse who? Me... or you?
Look inwards,
Touch skinwards,
Step sinwards.

I lullaby my son
While I daydream a different path,
And choose the one I'm on.

---

*A Chinese proverb says, "Another man's wife is often better, but
a man's own children are always best."*

Met Your Match

You woke and stretched,
And kissed
My shoulder.

You rose and dressed,
And looked
Much older.

Tall, beautiful, masculine.
Wonderful.

Your shirt was checked
And blue,
And warm.

Your belt was broad
And brown,
Like arms

Sensual, strong, scented.
Wonderful.

You smiled and purred
And circled
My waist.

We kissed and touched
Goodbye
In haste.

Soon. When, how, whether...
Wonderful.

For PJL.

• Lust

Midnight Oil

Your skin is as smooth
As midnight oil
To the tongue, to the touch.
But it pours on me
And troubles my waters.

No, Really, I Insist.

I'll help you pack.
I don't want to find that you come back
For anything you may have left behind
In error.
Especially
If it's me.
The terror
Of being alone
Has gone.

Phoenix

You can't catch a computer virus from a sneeze.
A floppy drive is not the same as a soft squeeze.
Humanity's about
Germs and sperms and spit.
The dirt and hurt are part of it.

"Sanitary" is not for kisses, it's for sissies.
Does creativity crave symmetry?
Ask Picasso
And Steven Hawking, while you're gawking
At her wet dream of a 3-foot inseam.

Take a walk on the wild side:
You won't find a mail-order child-bride.
These are called
Adult movies because these are grown-up games:
People with names and shames and blames;

We're humans who've been down in flames
And we've risen like a phoenix:
Older, balder,
Scarred and charred,
But unafraid to burn.

Pressing the Flesh

These political parades:
Pursed lips, dry palms,
Powdered cheeks and proffered babes
Are weak, nerveless excuses
For pressing the flesh.

It means
More than a handshake.
It's slaking a lustful thirst
With mouthfuls of fresh juice
From the nearest femme fountain
Or
With dewdrops from the summit
Of a man-mountain.
And it's cheek-by-jowl crowding
With the rank reek of squalor and sweat
Making all men wet in equal measure...
That's pressing the flesh.

Skin was made for sin.
For living in,
For touching,
Trying and
Giving in.

That's pressing the flesh.

Pushing Me Away

I
Afraid
Of getting any closer,
Nearer,
Dearer,
Only to find it was a dreadful mistake.

To see
In my reflection
Rejection,
Abnegation.
My face festooned with damaged dreams.

II
"You're pushing me away," you said.
"You're twisting all the thoughts inside my head."

But I'm not.

I'm running, helter-skelter,
For the spot
Where I left my bomb-shelter.

So I can dive

Head down, arse up;
Dive in
And stay alive.

It's fear of shrapnel,
Can't you tell?

Romeo of Essex

I wouldn't feel so badly
If she'd looked great
And I'd seen your skin twitching,
Itching,
Burning for the ultimate hot date.

But it dissolves me in my own acid
To be so invisible
Next to something so plain, to sex so
Essex,
So infinitely risible.

If it was silken words, like precious
Birds—her gifts of speech
Turning your head and lowering your
Standards
(And your pants)—but that wasn't it.

She was just... there. Lips and legs
Akimbo. I was passed over
For a bimbo. And worse... She's my friend.
There it is,
The clever twist at the end of the plot.

Hot Essex sex, cold as ice.
You chose her over me
Before you even knew
She was nice.

• Lust

Seven

He unpicked me
    ... Stitch by stitch

And my grievances mounted
    ... Bitch by bitch

And the urge to leave strengthened
    ... Itch by itch

Till I stated
my case,
Packed
my case,
And left him
with a bad case
Of missing me.

She

She
Has a tinkly laugh
(The kind that boys who should know better still like).
She
Has a pert bum
(The kind that looks good perched on a motorbike).
She
Has long, straight hair that's really shiny.
She
Has covetous eyes that want what's mine.
She
Has thighs, when she stands, that leave space between them
And
Nails so white, she must constantly clean them. And
She
Wants what I've got. (If I'm wrong, then sue me.)
But when he's around
She
Looks straight through me.

Soundings

Daily I find your disposable corneas
Abandoned on the loo seat or
The bathroom counter.

I love you to the depths of distraction
But even this Titanic adoration
Could one day founder

On the rocks of single socks,
The sandbanks of hanks of plughole hair,
The icebergs of can't be bothered.

Stevie P

You bedded me warmly
And wedded me to your soul
With brush of eyelash tip,
Soft-bitten lip.

You laughed
And my world laughed with you;
You cried
And I cradled your heart.

You bade me farewell
And left me a skyline to sit in—
With thoughts of warm hands,
Reunions, wedding bands.

You laughed
And my world laughed with you;
You cried
And I cradled your heart.

• Lust

Stitch in Time

Knit one, purl one,
Drop stitch, unravel.

Bickering's sickening
Fighting's frightening
Anger's angled

Like separated needles.

Resolution's restful
Compromises successful
Love's uneventful.

Knit one, purl one,
Knit one, purl one,
Knit one, purl one,
Knit one, purl one,
Knit one, purl one,
Knit one, purl one,
Knit one, purl one,
Knit one, purl one,
Knit one, purl one,
Knit one, purl one,
Knit one, purl one,
Knit one, purl one,
Knit one, purl one,
Knit one, purl one,
Knit one, purl one,
Knit one, purl one,
Knit one, purl one,
Knit one, purl one,
Knit one, purl one,
Knit one, purl one...

(Boring, isn't it?)

Strawberries (Pick Your Own)

He looks her right in the eye.
No-one here could claim to be shy,
Or not to know *exactly* why:
"Say 'strawberry' for me," he asks.
This is a game for grown men,
And
The woman laughs, low and throatily.

She murmurs the word. Juice drips
Into his ears from her licked lips;
His hands rest lightly on her hips.
This should be the season
For grown-up good sense,
But
This unreason is ripe with possibility.

Each
Awakes, alone,
Smiling and stretching
Amidst the scent of forbidden fruit.

For MMM.

Strength, Courage and Faerie Magick

You said you believed the movies.
You said romance is real life.
Will you stand while your feet set in concrete
Or scale a cliff up to the light?

They can't run into the sunset
Wearing boots that are lined with lead,
And if they stop to ponder consequence,
Chance, running barefoot, has fled.

So they juggle with the aftermath
They create as they go along,
While everyone tells them that love at
First sight's just a lyric in a song.

Cold water will bring out your bruises.
If you jump, you could thud back to Earth.
Good sense always hands us an ice pack,
A script rolls in cool, breaking surf.

Of all the bars in all the world
You had to walk into mine.
It's a movie scenario, we write the script
And it's shooting in real-time.

Sun-Kissed

Wake up, my lovely:
The sun is kissing your beautiful face
And the clouds play a smile on your lips.
Wake up, my lovely,
Share the beauty of a world we'll both learn,
Feel the breeze, cool, on the warmth of our love.

Walk with me, lovely,
Smell the greenness of this special day.
Take me in your arms and let's float away.
Run with me, lovely,
We'll head for the honey-tinged sunset
And believe in a life-lasting love.

Dream with me, lovely,
As the blue velvet night wraps us round,
As the moon drops its buttercup petals.
Lay with me, lovely,
Hold me close to your heart-beating body
Kiss my eyelids to sleep with your love.

Sweat

Sweat runs
Like your fingernail
Between my breasts

And then,
Like your hand, on my
Belly rests—

Testing my nerve.
It serves
No purpose
To remove it.
You remain unmoved.

Time slides,
Like a hungry snail
Until you leave.

Judgement? Reserved.
It serves
No purpose
To ask you to stay.
You refuse, unmoved.

Sweet Oblivion

There is a tropical rainforest, a jewel in a distant land,
And its name shall be called "Sweet Oblivion"
And its fate is in your hand.

A sweet, dew-dropped humidity; a steam scenting of
honey;
Its populace, Birds of Paradise,
Are seen for love, not money.

Within this hedonistic Utopia, lie seeds that can
regenerate;
In this succulent, dark incubator
A new Erewhon we shall create.

Eremite, hid in this jungle, having ventured 'cross hill
and savannah,
Let me show thee ephemeral beauty
And offer to thee Eros' manna.

See Jezebel dance with Madonna, 'neath a canopied
emerald silk,
While incarnadine stems sway together,
Come, partake of my honey and milk.

With your sensuous lips, seal our future; with your gaze
seek my secrets
And find my tropical rainforest, hidden
In recesses deep in your mind.

Taking Stock

I'm taking an inventory.
Recording every
Shade and hollow,
Hummock and ripple,
Ridge and curve.

I'm exploring your territory
Of desire, each
Sigh and gasp,
Goosebump and tremor
Touch and clench.

So if I ever need to, I can
Make a map
From memory.

The Elephant

She's not *exactly* smirking.
It's just that out of the corner of her eye
She keeps catching sight
Of an elephant in the room.

... And it's a very small room.

She'd cross her heart and swear
She saw it suddenly disappear behind
The strategically closed Venetian blind:
A pachyderm puff of smoke.

... And it's sending clear signals.

It happened when he stood to leave.
The creature chose to stage her reappearance
Through a doorway with marginal clearance.
Her bottom backing into the space.

... Nellie has entered the building (and is circus trained).

Nellie's forefoot on the girl's bare toes
Crushes like an embrace against a big man's bones;
Nellie's trunk brushes against her bottom, gone astray,
Like a man's hands brush a lock of hair away—

...Clearly, the action is a prelude to a passionate kiss...

But did either spot Nellie's immodest wink?
Lashes cast down in a knowing blink;
Eyelashes soft and long and fine
Like the downward slide of a zip on a spine...

... Maybe not. For at that moment...

• Lust

At the sight of fresh-peeled female,
At the moist exhalation of unfettered skin,
At the clearly articulated prospect of sin,
As the room became hot... and flushed... and hushed...

... Nellie blushed, and tiptoed quietly out.

The Jesus Stomp

Jesus!
You can't just wade in, thigh-deep
In bare feet,
And drop me down in
Close to drowning

Then walk out
Without
Leaving a ripple.

Jesus!
You invented an original sin,
Drew me in,
Spoke words more true
Than you intended to,

Then, genuflecting,
You saw
Your reflection.

Jesus!
Your rippled picture fractured;
Your catch
Lay abandoned—and what's more—
You simply headed for the sure.

Tommy Tucker

Now you sing for your succour,
Like everyone else.

The broad, beautiful back
To help bear up your burdens;
The arm-crook
Nestling head to soft breast;
Nuzzled neck
Smelling of sweet, familiar perfume—
All the old, priceless treasures
Now exact their toll;
Taken for granted
Becomes taken when granted.

Now you sing for your succour,
Like everyone else.

For BD.

Utterly Cowardly

You've made it up, this magic you talked about,
And now it's smeared over everything...

There are veils of lies drawn down over pairs of eyes
Too tired to see straight.

There are skeins of secret silk over which we've tripped
And realized too late.

There are strokes of skin vibrating to the notes of
Distant violins,

And one thousand jigsaw pieces which, complete, would
Picture all our sins.

There are beads of admiration shining lustrous as pearls
Around a stranger's neck.

There are consequences stacked like gambling chips
Beside a loaded deck.

And we've never even been lovers...

---

*For MM. The poem's title is also the title of a show in which I
performed in 1997. This was a collection of Noël Coward plays, of
which one was "We Were Dancing". The first and last lines of the
poem quote from this play.*

Velvet

I don't think you really know what colour hair I have.
It glows red in the sun,
And my eyes glow green,
And all I want is my share of the sunshine.

I don't think you can picture how bright I smile.
I light the Earth,
I pale the Sun.
But I guess I haven't smiled for a while.

I don't think you knew how rare a gem you wore.
You laid me down
And covered me with velvet,
Glanced away and were seduced by a costume pearl.

Watershed

"You smell of the watershed," you said.
"How so?" I asked
Still in the dark.
Maybe the drink
Had made you think.

But, shuffling across the sheets you told me:
"It divides North from West
And dry from wet.
It's where lives diverge
And lovers part."

"Is it a bad smell?" I queried, wearied.
"A sad smell..." you replied.
I sighed.
"... The smell of somewhere
Distant and melancholy".

• Lust

Zizz

She sizzled her way to the core of the party,
Her neckline ever-so-slightly tarty,
Her hail-fellow-well-met high fives hearty,
And outside she was glowing.

All heads turned to her, hot and flirty,
Her infectious laugh so deep and dirty,
And if other women felt slightly shirty?
Let them, she was glowing!

Two words whispered in her earringed ear:
She flashed straight back to late last year,
To jeans and trainers and paralysed fear...
But the light in her soul kept glowing.

ITCHY FEET

"This planet does not turn of its own accord; it is we who turn it with our gentle steps. A man must always move, for the earth requires it and a nomad knows that nature conspires in love."

—Danny Scheinmann
Random Acts of Heroic Love

Bali

Dawn from a balcony

I awake to a sky of kitchen-fire smoke and pearls
Lightening, brightening by cockerel crow degrees
To wafts of incense seen through an iridescent fishscale.

Morning in the garden

An azure light on dragonfly wings strikes like a gong;
Its song of strong sunlight is a rainbow
Longing for drops of sustaining rain.

Afternoon beneath the roof

Against hushed percussion of rain-tapped banana leaf,
My roof—masked ministerial red—drops diamonds;
And I remember that here we don't use religion as lipstick
And spirits travel always in straight lines.

Night of the Barong

From the slick street's star-spangled drenching I turn
To trace a path of darkened water, frangipani-strewn.
As lotus rises to meet penjor's pendulous, plaited pride
I am outside, in every sense, bleeding crimson
And gold of gamelan and dragonflowers, fringed Canopies
and stiff-collared children.
I am Bondress, the clown, snaggle-toothed and ignorant.

A Barong *(king of the good spirits) mask is worn for Balinese
ceremonial dances; the* penjor *is a ceremonial bamboo pole
decorated with coconut leaves and with an offering at the base.*
Bondress *is the clown in Balinese dance-drama.*
Menstruating women are excluded from Balinese temples.

Balicasag

Her rock-stubbed
Sand-worn
Toes,
The colour and shape
Of tiny sweet
Potatoes,
Seem rooted on
The plains of her rubber shoes.

She stands surveying:
No start to this
Sea,
Just a sudden change
From matte,
Flat horizon
To shifting,
Shimmering, burnished blues.

Bangkok

Click, click, click,
Click it.
Tear off a river bus ticket.

See the shore lights
Zig, zag, gold and bronze
Over river ripples reminiscent
Of dark woven sarongs.

Sunken sampan—
Under sunset
Under smog
And under waters full of lotus buds...
And dead dogs.

Dawn—
Streaked with oyster.
The moist, morning smog-mists.
Bangkok lifts
Its Naga heads.

Naga *is a sanskrit word for snake or dragon. In Thai* wats
*(temples) the Buddha is often depicted seated on a nine-headed
Naga throne.*

Concrete Bungle

I bet it was beautiful before they poured concrete on it.
I bet life here was great before it came pre-stressed.
I bet we could have had fun,
But our roles are pre-cast
And reinforced with steel.

Death Valley Sunset

Foot to the floor,
Flat,
I speed,
White with fright,
Awed by the might,
Into the purple prose of night.

Flames lick my back,
Roses
Furl
And blossom
To left and right;
I run for the purple prose of night.

In haze it watches my approach.
With cold flesh it embraces me;
Sunset pursues to grip me,
Trip me;
I flee the blood-red poetry.

Divercity

For all my life has given me,
The richness and diversity,
The power and the energy of
Love from my Great British family—
There is still a deep-set longing,
A need for some belonging.

I was born in Germany,
But German's not the word for me.
I love the Dutch, but there's so much
That isn't Netherlands in me.

In Cyprus, neither Turk nor Greek
Could offer me the home I seek.
And nor am I Australian,
Though I grew up beneath their sun.

So did my years of travel
Help me somehow to unravel
The secret of identity
Concealed within my culture3?

I roar with laughter,
To discover after
Twenty years
And untold tears

That I belong
In Hong Kong.

For LL, dear friend, mentor, and cross-cultural guru.

Frisco

I wish I could etch
These aspens into rock.

I long for the perfect simile,
Fishing the dark pools in me
To liken these lichens... to what?

Mottled shade, sharp tirade of squirrel,
Ochreous innards of stumped log,
Treacle black wetness of unstirred bog,
The bloodied, trembling rosehip:

Captured veindrip between twisted
Cabled coils of pewter bark.
Deepbubbled streamsound
Overlayered with liquid harmony.
Armoured banks of leaf mosaic and chipped slate.
Droplet varnish on green logs that bridge
The brackish, blackish swamp
From which silver twigs
And lemon-yellow grass emerge
Pale but victorious.
A wholesome completeness.

This land was made for the poet I'd love to be.

Frisco is a lovely little town in the Rocky Mountains, in Colorado, USA. I lived there for a few months one winter, in a tiny wooden cabin, with a gigantic dog for company.

Funeral Home

The scent of jasmine flowers
Floods the nostrils of the living.
The dead don't care,
Don't see
The bamboo carcasses of floral tributes
Poking damp, discoloured bones
Through their skins of
Purple orchids.

Above, the arclights on the scaffolds
Compete with the rising moon
And the tattered flags of
Shredded daylight.
After rain, the washed French navy sky
Is smooth as the wrong side of silk
And sequined with
Aeroplanes.

Below, there's a slophouse feeling
And the sweaty stench of stale streets
Under shophouse ceilings
Sticks to shoe soles.
The toxic concrete paths beg
To scour themselves clean with a
Coconut husk
Toiletbrush.

Around the block, on the evening breeze,
The poisoned liquorice taint of petrol and
Sewers cedes to the scent of
Jasmine flowers.
And poor, exhausted citizens wander home
Into their blocks of local lives, to burn out
Like candle stubs under
Soot-rimmed glass.

Gloria in Excelsis Mexico

Gloria in Excelsis Deo,
From gold leaf to tin foil.

Walls as deep as faith
Protect the pews, the portraits,
The hassocks and numbered scenes of crucifixion...
(And the bottle of Tabasco sauce burning red as a candle
On the altar of the Lord).

Peeping shamefaced
From behind the Confessional
A yellow plastic crate of empty Pepsi bottles.
A priest cuts through the motes swirled into his church
By the Mexican wind

And mutters dusty
Benedictions in this house of God,
While his confessing congregation
Wearies itself beyond the energies required to sin
In the palm groves, sorting dates and oranges.

Gold Rush

I never could quite force myself to
Desecrate the old mine buildings
Huddled, decaying, on the brown grass and quartzy rock.

Couldn't force my feet to
Take my mind's eye to the gape-netted windows
And face the certain shock

Of piles of dead miners—forty-niners—grinning at me:
Bone meal, bone idle now,
With 1848 tattooed upon each blank-eyed brow;

Teeth all rotted out except the gold ones...
The old ones always said
The only decent nuggets here were the ones inside a
miner's head.

The California gold rush began in 1848. Those who flocked there as gold-seekers came to be known as "forty-niners".

Golden Gate

I see the sun set
And slide,
Gently,
Over the smudged lip of my westerly globe.

I envision its warmth,
Caressing
The curve
Of the East, come morning;

My lover's hand, the curve of my breast.

Hong Kong Street Atlas

And yet, somehow, I've always loved it...

In Western, streets are full of spit and peacock feathers:
Eyes meet eyes of those who rummage where there's
Reams of paper brides, sweet dreams for boys who died.
But they'll all go up in smoke the day the cardboard
Lexus burns.

Centred in Central, denominations meet & money talks,
And in shiny, air-brushed skyways it can even walk.
While a mall wall away from glamour, there's crowd and
                                        clamour
And an array of naked rainbows lies spreadeagled on the
                                        road

Sham Shui Po has got it covered, buttoned and back-lit
It's bundled, bagged and bought before you knew you
                                        wanted it;
Scissors, paper, stone, bead, braid, transformer, phone...
You can hear the angels moan to see this trove of
                                        unnecessities.

Meanwhile, up on the Peak, the land has broken out in
                                        bricks and fountains—
An acne attack that blights the face of mountains:
Megaphones and flags, vinyl shoes and plastic bags
Glitter litter for the hordes of tours that wear away the
                                        dragon's back.

Land of the Loose Women

The heat.
The meat hanging
The banging
The smell.

The street.
The rain teeming
Skin steaming
Hard sell.

Flat ducks.
A phone ringing
Birds singing
Pell mell.

A job.
A life learning
Tides turning
Tram bell.

A hill.
The smog choking
Frog croaking
Koel.

A friend.
A green walking
Love talking
All's well.

For the wonderful, warm, open, accepting, creative, supportive dancers known as "Loose Women".

London: Saturday 10th

No money, life's still funny.
Gilded carriage; glitter barrage.
Sore feet; cold food to eat.
Smiles on faces; so many places.
Window shopping, big hints dropping.
Laughs in throats; cold without coats.
Close-up cuddles; direction muddles.
Long-distance walking, non-stop talking.
Really miss you, tiptoes kiss you.
Wave goodbye, go home and cry.

For IH.

Namu

Naked as birth,
As the ceremonial moments before my skirt
Enfolded me in the female fruitfulness of flower rooms,
I bathe and look back on my life.
I walk my journey from enamel basin to porcelain tub;
I have traveled from lake to lavatory,
And I flush with pride.

I met the gloriously coquettish Yang Erche Namu at the Hong Kong International Literary Festival years ago. I was inspired by her life story published as an English-language autobiography, "Leaving Mother Lake: A Childhood at the Edge of the World", co-written with anthropologist Christine Mathieu. Born August 1966 (same as me) in a traditional Mosuo ethnic village near Lugu Lake in northern Yunnan province, she now lives and works internationally.

Old Stoney Inn

Boarded up and clapped out.

And down the road a piece,
There's a coyote
Smeared on the blacktop,
Chuckling redly and looking vengeful.

Written on a Greyhound bus as we crossed Arizona.

One more morning

Root vegetables stacked
Fat end out,
Like terrified rabbit rumps,
Turning tail and fleeing, burrow-bound.

Slick cones of vanilla-white squid
And palest
Pork-pink chops lie prim beneath
Chickens, pendulum-hung, from punctured throats.

Shades of red bloody the scene,
Complementary
Colour-coded by the forest green,
And shinbone-sheen of the *bak choi* mountain.

Poh-poh taps ash from her
Fag end,
Safe in Buddhist certainty:
The paper offerings she flogs are not destined to burn for
her, just yet.

One more market morning.

---

*This was my contribution to the artists' protest at plans to
redevelop the Graham Street market in Central, Hong Kong. My
friends Mabel Sieh and Annie Knibb translated it into Chinese and
overlaid it on a piece of visual art so we could create handouts to
give to stallholders and shoppers in the market.*
Bak choi—*a Chinese vegetable.*
Poh-poh—*grandma.*

Shanghai'd

Spittle glitters on the textured tiles of pathways for the
blind
That start and stop without a thought, with no reason or
rhyme.
It's charity, but curbed: dug up, concreted, cratered and
kerbed—all
In the race to scrape the sky and top it with a ball.

I hear there *is* a vision lurking in some daily-dusted
room,
But on these streets it's lost beneath success's sonic
boom.
The tracer fire of traffic sparks and arcs and strafes each
street,
While a chandelier hangs, theatrically, suspended in
disbelief:

Needing nothing but applause it hovers, full of light, not
sound,
An inverse tower of glass to reach from heaven to the
ground.
It blinks at the surrounding sprawl: incredible, dramatic
difference;
The warp and weft of theft so deft, that most remain
indifferent.

A hard crystal heart for this capital-rich, not-the-capital
city,
Towered over by robber barons who live without one tael
of pity.
An unforgiving river of renminbi flows by, rippling and
rank;
Gilt not guilt, and bonds not bunds now define and
shape its banks.

• Itchy Feet

No stitch in time to save a thing for the city's traditional
                                                    tailors—
Pudong's weight of expectation will turn them all to
                                                    sailors—
For as it sinks, obese, into its own grand declamations,
The tide casts history adrift on the debris of reclamation.

Sydney Sunset

Flashing green metronome
Heaving,
Gently
Breasting the rolling pewter swell.

A buoy, to light true passage
Through the charcoal hills
Beneath the dove-grey slurs of cloud—
Rumours of rain—their soft pink bellies exposed.

Lying shamelesly
(Like a choirboy's eyes)
Against a sky the same deep blue,
The sun drops to her knees in penance.

Ashen-faced sky,
Deceived suitor,
Gazes at her scarlet silks
Alas! Undone.

Timanfaya

Rhythm of rock,
Soft Earth's palpitation.
Deep in her belly:
Fire in the mountain.

Fertility made barren,
Green rendered black.
From tiny virgins of stone,
Life floods back.

---

*Timanfaya is a national park in Lanzarote, part of a UNESCO
biosphere reserve covering the whole volcanic island.*

Today

Today was a day, a perfect day
To sprawl, full-length
Upon the grass
And feel the strength
Of lush, green growth,
As dampness
Creeps through trouser legs.

Today was a day, an ideal day
To walk in the sun
Across the June-green park
And one by one
Take turns to plant
Soft kisses on each other's
Sun-warmed skin.

Touchdown: Pudong

My taxi's glass tints the sky a
Grubbier grey.
"Hint of Pollution" in a matte finish
Glossed over with a slick of rain.

So many poles and pylons,
Raised roads and peeling railings,
Pillars, walls and lamp-posts
Random lights and signposts;

Dystopian disorder on
Every street corner
Utter clutter:
A bad *Bladerunner*.

Features vie for notice,
Where's the unifying eye?
Then finally... Beyond... The Bund
Shanghai's grace and fervour.

Pudong is an area of Shanghai located on the east bank of the Huangpu River. On the opposite bank lies The Bund, with many buildings dating back to the 19th *century. "Bladerunner" is a 1982 film directed by Ridley Scott.*

Travelling Home

Sifu on the *siuba* sips a can of *cahsiba*
Clamped in a hand
The colour of a conker.

Jeje jokes with *sai-lo*, leaning so low
That I don't know
If they're giggling Chinese or Tagalog.

Mama's sick of her "*sik sau sin*" skin
So she sits on *sai teet*
Rubbing handcream in.

We pass *Jungjung* spreading grains of *faahn*
To dry out in the sun
Beside his garden of *gaai laan*.

My money-haired kids play *bauh-jin-dap*
In the courtyard below
With their black-haired best *pahngyauh*.

It's nice to be home.

The phonetic romanisation of Cantonese used here is my own:
Sifu—respectful term for a craftsman, e.g. a carpenter or builder.
Siuba—mini-bus. Cahsiba—Carlsberg beer. Jeje—big sister (often
used to refer to a domestic helper). Sai-lo—little brother. Sik Sau
Sin—"Wash hands first", a government campaign slogan to
encourage domestic hygiene. Sai teet—West Rail. Jungjung—
Grandpa. Faahn—rice. Gai Laan—a green vegetable. Bauh-Jin-
Dap—the game Rock, Paper, Scissors. Pahngyauh—friend.
"Money-haired"— Traditional Chinese people can see blonde hair
as gold in colour (representing wealth or fortune); so they like to
touch my children's heads.

Walking Old Tollbooth Wynd

Grandpa's legs are too old and slow to
Climb the steps into the cemetery.
Grandson jokes: "Only way he'll get there's if we carry
him!"

Grandpa smiles cheerily, and waves:
"Go on up..." Then thinks, eerily,
I can take all day and I'll still see the grave before you.

Old Tollbooth Wynd is a street in Edinburgh, Scotland.

We ♥ Hong Kong

It's the love affair
You knew you'd never marry:
The one that laughed the loudest,
Kissed the softest,
Had the hottest sex.

It's the love affair
Of yin and yang imperfection
A sweet fruit hiding the seeds
Of something wrong.
It's Hong Kong.

Westcliff-on-Sea

Here's a postcard from Southend—
One I don't intend,
Or need, to stamp and send.

There's a stretch of sand
Designed for two, and
Strolling romantically, hand-in-hand.

There are old seafront hotels,
And knick-knacks made of shells,
And wave-washed seaweed smells.

Here's a note from the seaside
To say I'd
Like to have you by my side...

Wish you were here.

Winged

I watch the wave of frigate birds
Over ocean water—
Once, twice, thrice.
Shallow W of wings,
They slice, slim as rice sickles,
Through thin air.

It is an offering to all the gods,
To feel this awestruck emotion.

This is my daily devotion:
To witness these—
Unnerving in their perfection,
Unswerving in their dedication
To worship
The Balinese breeze.

• Itchy Feet

Wolfie's: Miami Beach

Still caught in the warp
When they cruised the strip:
Brown suit, brown shirt, brown kipper tie.
He leans towards her, his chat at the ready.
Barbie doll behind the chrome and formica counter
Smiling, and softly curled;

Perky as her coffee
(But not as fresh, after sixty years),
Bright as the urn, she talks to Wolfie with a
Tongue as sharp as the jarred pickled cabbage—
She, and the gay Spanish waiter, and "God,
He's such a flirt."

Yosemite

I am scaling a fang
As sheer as a wall:
Immense
White
Masticator of
Manna from Heaven

If you folded this nation in half,
Hingeing
From Texas through Nebraska to North Dakota,
The west would chaw tobacco
And grin its stained Californian toothy smile,
While
The east would suck and slurp and burp
Gummily on sea-salt saliva.

Yosemite is a UNESCO World Heritage site in California. It includes the granite cliffs that form part of the western slopes of the Sierra Nevada mountain

Early Responses to Wonder, Lust & Itchy Feet

"Poetry looks straight at what the rest of us leave in the periphery of our vision: Sally Dellow, again and again, brings back our lazy eye to focus, precisely, on the nub of experience. Exuberant word-play and a singing ear bring music and humour to all that she scrutinises. There's beautiful stuff here: a lovely woman who lays her bodies bare in all her lives and roles, then looks the reader squarely in the eye — and grins. Surprising us with 'waters full of lotus buds ... / And dead dogs', Dellow is raucous, irreverent and achingly naked. This collection is all tender warmth and wonder, but hilarious and 'Hot as Wasabi' too."
— **Martin Alexander**, author of *Clearing Ground* and Poetry Editor of the *Asia Literary Review*

"These are generous and intimate poems, crafted with language that dances on the page, borne out of keen observation and contemplation of not only life's most joyous moments, but also its most sorrowful, and at times, most frightening."
— **David W. Hill**, Fiction Writer and Assistant Editor of *Underground America: Narratives of Undocumented Lives*

"Evocative yet compact in its language, Sally Dellow's collection reveals a desire to grasp poetry—and life—by the horns. By turns lucid and playful, these poems are characterised by a humour and lightness of touch that enable both writer and reader to engage with issues that matter. In 'Mottled', she sets out her perception of poetry as 'hard thoughts softened by beautiful constructs; // Sweet sounds wrapped round pain'. There is much pain, much sweetness to be found within these pages."
— **Viki Holmes**, author of *miss moon's class,* and co-editor of the international women's poetry anthology *Not a Muse*

"With an artist's eye, Sally Dellow looks at key aspects of life—the search for a home, the need for companionship, the satisfaction of family—and finds something amazing in each remembered detail. She selects scenes from her experience as a traveler, mother and writer, and presents them with an immediacy that allows us to share in the moment. Each poem in this collection contains vivid images, unexpected turns of phrase, and insight into what it means to be aware, worldly and human in the present day."
— **Thaddeus Rutkowski**, author of *Haywire*

"*Wonder, Lust & Itchy Feet* is an intimate journey; the emotional vulnerability gives the pieces their veracity. Tellingly, many Hong Kong poems in the Itchy Feet section declare an unavowed commitment to the place that she has made her home. Perhaps she has scratched that particular itch for the last time."
— **David McKirdy**, author of *Accidental Oriental*

SOME POETRY AND POETRY COLLECTIONS
Published by Proverse Hong Kong

Astra and Sebastian, by L.W. Illsley. 2011.

Bliss of Bewilderment, by Birgit Bunzel Linder. 2017.

Chasing light, by Patricia Glinton Meicholas. 2013.

China suite and other poems, by Gillian Bickley. 2009.

For the record and other poems of Hong Kong,
   by Gillian Bickley. 2003.

Frida Kahlo's cry and other poems,
   by Laura Solomon. 2015.

Home, away, elsewhere, by Vaughan Rapatahana. 2011.

Immortelle and bhandaaraa poems,
   by Lelawattee Manoo-Rahming. 2011.

In vitro, by Laura Solomon. 2nd ed. 2014.

Irreverent poems for pretentious people,
   by Henrik Hoeg. 2016.

*Mingled voices: the international Proverse Poetry Prize
anthology 2016*,
   edited by Gillian and Verner Bickley. 2017.

*Mingled voices, 2: the international Proverse Poetry Prize
anthology 2017*,
   edited by Gillian and Verner Bickley. 2018.

Moving house and other poems from Hong Kong,
   by Gillian Bickley. 2005.

Of leaves & ashes, by Patty Ho. 2016.

Of symbols misused, by Mary-Jane Newton. 2011.

Over the Years: Selected Collected Poems, 1972-2015,
    by Gillian Bickley. 2017.

Painting the borrowed house: poems,
    by Kate Rogers. 2008.

Perceptions, by Gillian Bickley. 2012.

Rain on the pacific coast, by Elbert Siu Ping Lee. 2013.

refrain, by Jason S. Polley. 2010.

Shadow play, by James Norcliffe. 2012.

Shadows in deferment, by Birgit Bunzel Linder. 2013.

Shifting sands, by Deepa Vanjani. 2016.

*Sightings: a collection of poetry, with an essay,
'communicating poems'*, by Gillian Bickley. 2007.

Smoked pearl: poems of Hong Kong and beyond,
    by Akin Jeje (Akinsola Olufemi Jeje). 2010.

The layers between (essays and poems),
    by Celia Claase. 2015.

Unlocking, by Mary-Jane Newton. March 2014.

Violet, by Carolina Ilica. March 2019.

Wonder, lust & itchy feet, by Sally Dellow. 2011.

• Itchy Feet

FIND OUT MORE ABOUT OUR AUTHORS, BOOKS, EVENTS AND LITERARY PRIZES

Visit our website: http://www.proversepublishing.com
Visit our distributor's website:
<www.chineseupress.com>

Follow us on Twitter
Follow news and conversation: twitter.com/Proversebooks>
OR
Copy and paste the following to your browser window and
follow the instructions:
https://twitter.com/#!/ProverseBooks

"Like" us on www.facebook.com/ProversePress
Request our free E-Newsletter
Send your request to info@proversepublishing.com.

Availability
Most titles are available in Hong Kong and world-wide
from our Hong Kong based Distributor,
The Chinese University of Hong Kong Press, The Chinese
University of Hong Kong,
Shatin, NT, Hong Kong SAR, China.
Email: cup-bus@cuhk.edu.hk
Website: <www.chineseupress.com>.

All titles are available from Proverse Hong Kong,
http://www.proversepublishing.com

Stock-holding retailers
Hong Kong (Bookazine), Singapore (Select Books),
Canada (Elizabeth Campbell Books),
Andorra (Llibreria La Puça, La Llibreria).

Orders from bookshops in the UK and elsewhere.

Ebooks
Many of our titles are available also as Ebooks.

www.ingramcontent.com/pod-product-compliance
Lightning Source LLC
Chambersburg PA
CBHW062108080426
42734CB00012B/2792